America, My Country
Explorers

Henry Hudson

By Moira Rose Donohue

Clarke C. Scott, M.A.
Content Consultant

STATE STANDARDS PUBLISHING

Your State • Your Standards • Your Grade Level

Dear Educators, Librarians and Parents . . .

Thank you for choosing this *"America, My Country"* book! We have designed this series to support state Departments of Educations' Common Core Standards for curriculum studies AND leveled informational text. Each book in the series has been written at grade level as measured by the ATOS Readability Formula for Books (Accelerated Reader), the Lexile Framework for Reading, and the Fountas & Pinnell Benchmark Assessment System for Guided Reading. Images, captions, and other design and critical thinking elements provide supportive visual messaging and learning activities to enhance text comprehension. Glossary and Word Index sections introduce key new words and help young readers develop skills in locating and combining information. We wish you all success in using this *"America, My Country"* series to meet your student or child's learning needs.

Jill Ward, President

Publisher

State Standards Publishing, LLC
1788 Quail Hollow
Hamilton, GA 31811
USA
1.866.740.3056
www.statestandardspublishing.com

Cataloging-in-Publication Data

Donohue, Moira Rose.
   Henry Hudson / Moira Rose Donohue.
      p. cm. -- (America, my country explorers)
   Includes index.
   ISBN 978-1-93881-316-0 (lib. bdg.)
   ISBN 978-1-93881-319-1 (pbk.)
   1. Hudson, Henry, -1611--Juvenile literature.   2. Explorers--America--Biography--
   Juvenile literature.   3. Explorers--Great Britain--Biography-- Juvenile literature.   I. Title.
   910.92--dc23
   [B]

2013947899

About the Author

Moira Rose Donohue has a Bachelor of Arts degree in political science from Mississippi University for Women and a Juris Doctorate degree from Santa Clara University School of Law. She was a banking legislative lawyer for 20 years before she began writing for children. Moira is a published author of numerous poems, plays, and articles, as well as two picture books. She loves dogs and tap dancing, and lives in northern Virginia with her family.

About the Content Consultant

Clarke C. Scott holds degrees from Central Michigan University and has 33 years of experience as a classroom teacher, building principal and system-wide administrator. Clarke most recently served as Director of Middle School Education and Lead Director for History with Pittsylvania County Schools in Virginia. He enjoys hiking, kayaking, caving, and exploring Virginia's and our nation's history. He shares his adventures both above and underground with his wife, Joyce, and family.

1 2 3 4 5 – CG – 18 17 16 15 14

Table of Contents

Hi, I'm Bagster!
Let's learn about
Explorers.

MY STATE

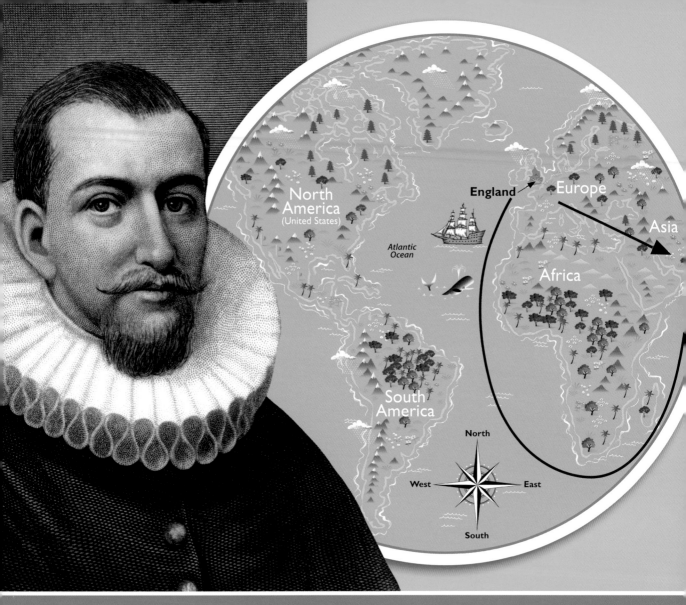

North America
(United States)

Atlantic
Ocean

England

Europe

Asia

Africa

South
America

North

West

East

South

In Henry Hudson's day, people wanted spices from southern Asia, but traveling was slow and unsafe.

Man of Mystery

Henry Hudson was born in Europe in the country of England. Historians think he was born around 1570, but no one knows exactly when. In fact, no one knows much at all about Henry's life before he went to sea for the first time. Henry grew up somewhere in the city of London. Historians believe Henry's grandfather was also named Henry Hudson. Grandpa Henry helped start a trading company in England called the Muscovy Company.

In Henry's day, people wanted spices from southern Asia. Spices kept food fresh and made it taste better. These items were **scarce**, or hard to find, in Europe. But traveling to Asia by land was slow and unsafe. So was sailing to Asia around Africa. Many people believed there was a **Northwest Passage** to Asia, across the Atlantic Ocean. The Muscovy Company hoped to find the passage.

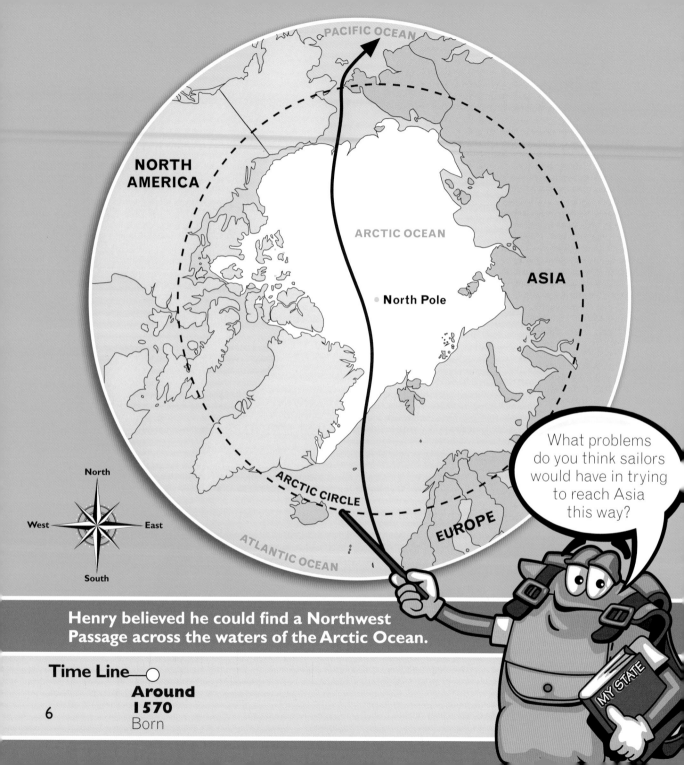

What problems do you think sailors would have in trying to reach Asia this way?

Henry believed he could find a Northwest Passage across the waters of the Arctic Ocean.

Time Line

Around 1570
Born

Pole Vault

Historians don't know where Henry went to school. But he did learn to read and write, and to fish and sail. Henry may have sailed to the **New World** with English **explorer** John Davis. Europeans called the Americas the New World. Henry also learned how to **navigate**, or set a ship's course. Back then, explorers used a **compass** and the stars to figure out the ship's direction. A compass finds direction with a magnetic needle and always points to the **North Pole**, the most northern point of the earth.

Henry married a woman named Katherine. They had three sons named Richard, John, and Oliver. One day, Henry got an idea about finding the Northwest Passage. He believed he could sail to Asia across the waters of the Arctic Ocean—sailing over the top of the world! He thought that the long days of summer melted the ice there, so ships could sail through.

Europeans called the Americas the New World.

The crew slept in hanging beds called hammocks.

Henry found many whales off the shore of Spitsbergen.

Time Line

Around
1570
Born

1607
Sails to
Spitsbergen

Journey 1 – Blubber

The Muscovy Company decided to let Henry prove his idea and gave him a ship called the *Hopewell*. Henry set sail from London on April 23, 1607, but he ran into bad weather and had to pull into another port. He finally left England on May 1st. Henry's son, John, was a cabin boy. The ship was small and crowded. The crew slept in hanging beds called hammocks.

In June, Henry saw the coast of Greenland, which is called Kalaallit Nunaat by the people there today. Then he sailed northeast to the island of Spitsbergen, which is now part of Norway. The *Hopewell* ran into a surprise. "In this bay we saw many whales . . ." wrote Henry. Back then, whale fat, called blubber, was used for lamp oil. People used other parts of the whale to make clothing and even perfume! Whaling became a big industry in England, and whales were prized.

The North Pole is dark for six months out of the year.

The *Hopewell* became blocked by ice, like this ship.

Would you want to explore the Arctic Ocean? Why or why not?

Time Line

Around **1570**
Born

1607
Sails to
Spitsbergen

10

MY STATE

Journey 2 – Ice!

The ship continued to sail north into the Arctic Ocean. Soon, ice blocked its path. Henry didn't know it, but he was only about 600 miles from the North Pole. The North Pole is dark for six months out of the year, and the ice never melts. Henry had been wrong about the ice melting. Now he had to turn the ship around.

When Henry got back to England in September, he told the Muscovy Company he had not reached Asia. But he also told them good news—he had found whales. The Muscovy Company knew that it could hunt whales and become rich. But Henry still wanted to reach Asia. The Muscovy Company agreed to send him exploring again, but this time he would travel northeast. In April 1608, Henry set sail with a crew of fourteen, including his son, John. Henry picked a man named Robert Juet to be his first mate.

It's a Fact!

Over the years, many countries, including the United States, hunted whales. Sadly, many types of whales almost became **extinct**—they almost died out due to overhunting.

Henry and his crew thought they saw a mermaid!

Time Line

Around 1570
Born

1607
Sails to Spitsbergen

1608
Sails to Russia

Mermaid or Manatee?

This time, Henry began looking for a **Northeast Passage** to Asia through the Arctic Ocean. He sailed north beyond Norway, and then east toward Russia. Before long, Henry found himself sailing around icebergs. Icebergs are dangerous—they can sink a ship, like the *Titanic*. Soon, Henry reached Novaya Zemlya, a group of islands in Russia. The crew thought they saw a mermaid! Some people think it may have been a manatee. Maybe it was. But manatees only live in warm, shallow waters.

In July, the ship hit storms and more ice, so Henry changed course. Instead of sailing east, he decided to sail west to the New World. But the crew wanted to go back to England. Historians think that Robert Juet told Henry that the crew was going to **mutiny**, or take over the ship. Henry had no choice. He sailed home.

It's a Fact!

The manatee is a large mammal that lives in shallow coastal waters. It is sometimes called a sea cow but is related to the elephant. It can eat 1/10th of its weight in 24 hours. Do you think a manatee looks like a mermaid?

Henry set sail on the *Half Moon* to look for the Northeast Passage.

Henry turned around and sailed west to look for the Northwest Passage again.

Time Line

Around 1570 Born	1607 Sails to Spitsbergen	1608 Sails to Russia	1609 Sails for Holland

Journey 3 – Henry Goes Dutch

The Muscovy Company didn't want to send Henry on any more journeys. He had not found a path to Asia. So Henry went to work for the Dutch East India Company in Holland. Holland is part of the Netherlands today, and the people there are called the Dutch. The Dutch East India Company gave Henry a small ship called the *Half Moon* to look for the Northeast Passage. In April 1609, Henry set sail for Novaya Zemlya again. He took his son, John. He also took Robert Juet again, even though Robert had caused trouble on the trip before.

Henry ran into a problem on the way. Can you guess what it was? Ice! So Henry turned around and sailed west to look for the Northwest Passage again. This time, his crew agreed. But Henry had more trouble. His contract with the Dutch East India Company said Henry had to return to Holland if he couldn't find a Northeast Passage. But Henry had other ideas.

It's a Fact!

The Netherlands is famous for windmills, wooden shoes, and tulips. Tulips come in almost 4,000 types.

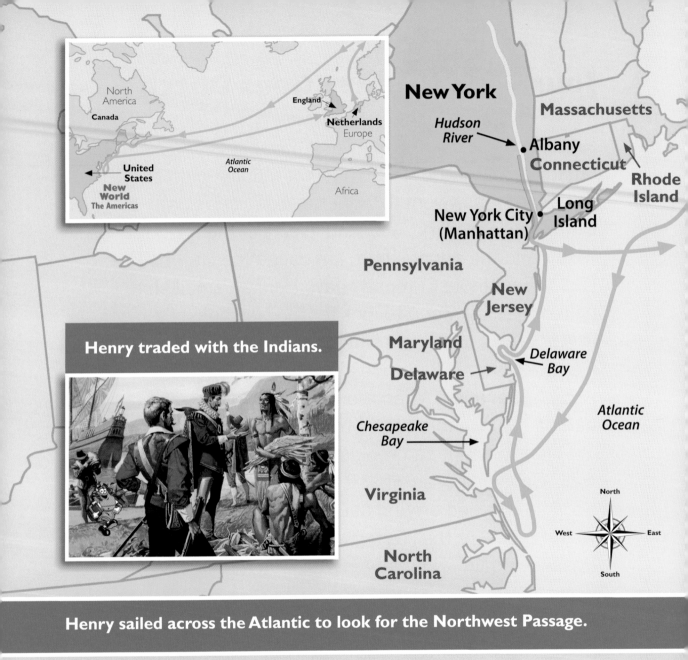

North America

Canada

England

Netherlands
Europe

United States
New World
The Americas

Atlantic Ocean

Africa

New York

Hudson River → • Albany

Massachusetts

Connecticut

New York City • (Manhattan)

Long Island

Rhode Island

Pennsylvania

New Jersey

Maryland

Delaware → *Delaware Bay*

Chesapeake Bay →

Atlantic Ocean

Virginia

North Carolina

North
West East
South

Henry traded with the Indians.

Henry sailed across the Atlantic to look for the Northwest Passage.

Time Line

| Around **1570** Born | **1607** Sails to Spitsbergen | **1608** Sails to Russia | **1609** Sails for Holland |

New York, New York!

Henry disobeyed the contract and sailed across the Atlantic. He reached present-day Canada and sailed south. He passed two large bodies of water—the Chesapeake Bay and Delaware Bay. But he didn't find a Northwest Passage. He sailed farther north around New Jersey and in between several islands. He came upon a great river that led him to tiny Manhattan Island. Henry traded with the Indians there, then he sailed up the river to present-day Albany, New York. That didn't lead to a Northwest Passage either. Henry claimed the area for Holland but then sailed back to England. Why didn't he return to Holland? Was he afraid to face the Dutch because he had disobeyed? Or was he an English spy? Some historians think so. They think Henry took maps from the Dutch to give to England.

It's a Fact!

New York City began on Manhattan Island as a Dutch colony called New Amsterdam, after the capital of the Netherlands. The Lenape Indians let the Dutch share the island for trade goods worth about $35 in today's money. The Dutch thought they were buying Manhattan.

The crew abandoned Henry and his friends and sailed home without them.

Time Line

| Around 1570 Born | 1607 Sails to Spitsbergen | 1608 Sails to Russia | 1609 Sails for Holland | 1610 Returns to New World |

Journey 4 – Disappearing Act

When Henry got to England, soldiers took him to London to see King James I of England. Henry was in trouble. King James was mad that Henry had claimed land in the New World for Holland. He put Henry under arrest. But some important tradesmen in England convinced the king to free Henry. They raised money to give Henry a ship called the *Discovery*. They believed he could find the Northwest Passage. Henry sailed on the *Discovery* in April 1610. Again, he took his son, John, and Robert Juet along.

The *Discovery* sailed back to the New World. Henry explored a large bay and other bodies of water in Canada. This time, Henry claimed the area for England. But soon, icy waters trapped the ship. The crew had to spend the winter in Canada. In the spring, the men wanted to go home, but Henry said, "No." So Robert Juet planned a mutiny. This time, with the help of others, he carried it out. In June 1611, the crew put Henry, his son, and Henry's friends into a small boat. They **abandoned** Henry. The *Discovery* sailed home without them.

Hudson River

Hudson River

Hudson Strait

Hudson Bay

Canada

Hudson River

United States

Atlantic Ocean

The river Henry sailed from New York City to Albany is called the Hudson River

Time Line

20

| Around 1570 Born | 1607 Sails to Spitsbergen | 1608 Sails to Russia | 1609 Sails for Holland | 1610 Returns to New World | 1611 Died? |

What's in a Name?

Henry was never heard from again. Did he die at sea? Or did he make it to land? His death is as much a mystery as his early life. Some historians think Henry landed in Canada because of a rock found there with "HH CAPTIVE 1612" carved in it. The *Discovery* returned to England, but Robert Juet died on the way. Sometime later, the rest of the crew was charged with mutiny, but they were never punished.

Henry had a talent for finding trouble. He had a talent for finding ice. But he also had a talent for exploring and mapping new places. Today, the river he sailed from New York City to Albany is called the Hudson River. And the large bay he explored in Canada is called Hudson Bay. Bridges, schools, and other waterways, such as the Hudson Strait, are named after him, too.

Canada's Hudson Bay is named after Henry.

Glossary

abandon – To leave someone or something behind and never return.

compass – A tool that finds direction using a magnetic needle pointing to the North Pole.

explorer – A person who travels seeking new discoveries.

extinct – A species of plants or animals that has died out and no longer exists.

mutiny – To refuse to obey orders; or to turn against a person in charge.

navigate – To set the course, or direction, of a ship.

New World – The name Europeans called the Americas. The New World includes the continents of North America and South America.

North Pole – The most northern point of the earth.

Northeast Passage – A pathway across the Arctic Ocean and other waters that allows sailors to travel northeast from Europe to Asia.

Northwest Passage – A pathway across the Atlantic Ocean that allows sailors to travel northwest from Europe to Asia.

scarce – Not plentiful. Something that is in short supply or hard to find.

Say these words like a pro!

Sound It Out!

Kalaallit Nunaat: **kah-lah-leet noo-naht**

Lenape: **leh-nah-pay**

Muscovy: **mus-coh-vee**

Novaya Zemlya: **noh-va-yah zim-lee-ah**

Robert Juet: **joo-et**

Spitsbergen: **spitz-burr-gehn**

Word Index

Editorial Credits

Designer: Michael Sellner, Corporate Graphics, North Mankato, Minnesota
Consultant/Marketing Design: Alison Hagler, Basset and Becker Advertising, Columbus, Georgia

Image Credits — *All images © copyright contributor below unless otherwise specified. Maps: Edward Grajeda/iStockphoto unless otherwise specified.*

Explore With Bagster

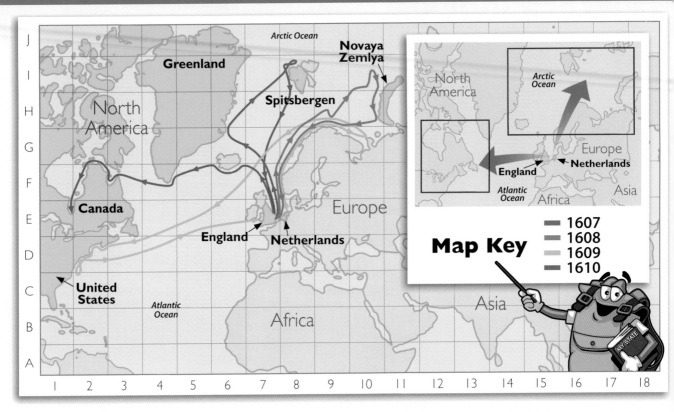

Map Key
- 1607
- 1608
- 1609
- 1610

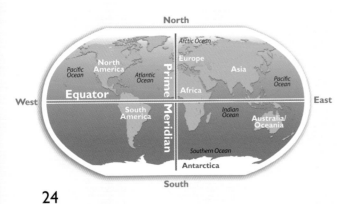

Words You Should Know!

continent – One of the great divisions of land on the earth. The seven continents are: Africa, Antarctica, Asia, Australia/Oceania, Europe, North America, and South America.

equator – An imaginary line around the center of the earth that divides the Northern Hemisphere from the Southern Hemisphere.

hemisphere – Half of a sphere (the globe) created by the equator or the prime meridian. The four hemispheres are: Northern, Southern, Western, and Eastern.

ocean – A vast body of salt water. The five oceans are: Arctic, Atlantic, Indian, Pacific, and Southern.

prime meridian – An imaginary line around the center of the earth that divides the Western Hemisphere from the Eastern Hemisphere.